THE
FACTS ABOUT
HINDUISM

Alison Cooper

WAYLAND

This book is based on the original title *Hinduism* by
Anita Ganeri, in the *What do we know about...?* series,
published in 1995 by Macdonald Young Books

This differentiated text version by Alison Cooper,
published in 2004 by Wayland
This paperback edition published in 2007
Reprinted 2008

Original designer and illustrator: Celia Hart
Layout for this edition: Jane Hawkins
Consultant: Dr Fatma Amer

Hachette Children's Books
338 Euston Road, London NW1 3BH

Photograph acknowledgements: Ancient Art & Architecture Collection, p17
(tl); The Bridgeman Art Library, London, endpapers (British Library, London)
pp38 (Freud Museum, London), 39(t) (Victoria and Albert Museum, London);
CIRCA Photo Library, pp9, 15(t), 17(b), 27(I); Dinodia/Tripp, pp21(t), 32(r),
35(c), 43; Robert Harding Picture Library, pp12(I), 20(I) (Tony Gervia), 32(I)
(JH Wilson), 35(t), 35(b) (JHC Wilson), 41(b); Michael Holford, pp13(b), 14,
16; The Hutchison Library, pp31(b), 33(r) (MacIntyre), 37; Magnum, pp15(b)
(Raghu Rai), 26 (Abbas); Bipinchandra J Mistry, p28(r); Chris Oxlade, p36(I);
Ann & Bury Peerless, pp13(t), 12(r), 18, 19(t) (br), 21(b), 22, 25(t), 27(r),
28(I), 29(t) (b), 31(c), 34, 36(r), 39(b), 42; Rex Features/Sipa-Press, p31(t);
Peter Sanders, pp23(t), 24, 25(b); Spectrum Colour Library, p40; Tony Stone
Images, pp8(I) (Anthony Cassidy), 8(r), 41(t) (David Hanson); Tripp, pp20(r)
(Helene Rogers), 23(b) (Helene Rogers), 30 (W Jacobs), 33 (I) (Helene Rogers).

All possible care has been taken to trace the ownership of each photograph
and to obtain permission for its use. If there are any omissions or if any errors
have occurred, they will be corrected in subsequent editions, on notification to
the Publishers.

Printed in China

A CIP catalogue record for this book is available
from the British Library

ISBN-13: 978 0 7502 5106 8

Endpapers: This painting shows a scene from the
Ramayana, in which Rama and Sita are living in
exile in the forest.

CONTENTS

WHO ARE THE HINDUS?

Hindus are followers of a religion called Hinduism. Hinduism began in India thousands of years ago and it is one of the oldest religions in the world. Hindus themselves call their religion *sanatana dharma* which means 'eternal law' or 'eternal teaching'. Although most Hindus live in India, many have moved to other countries, such as Britain. There are also some Hindus who are not from Indian families.

◀ **Holy man**
This holy man is a *sannyasin* (monk) who has left home in search of God. Holy men are often called *sadhus*. They give up all their possessions and wander from place to place praying and meditating.

▲ **Hindu temple**
This Hindu temple is in Bali, Indonesia, showing how Hinduism has spread far from India.

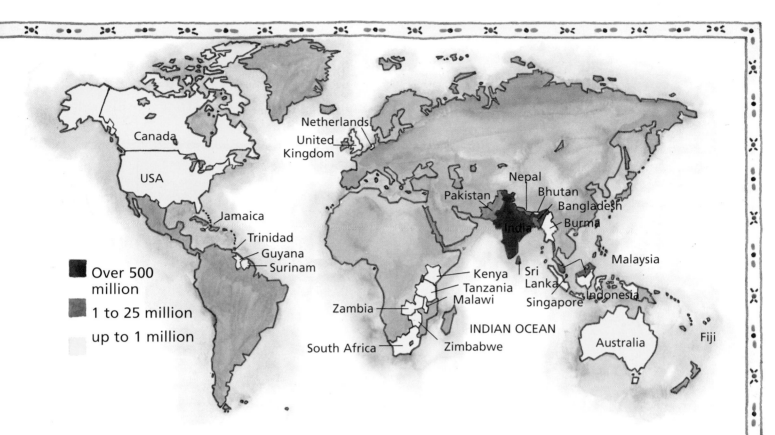

Over 500 million

1 to 25 million

up to 1 million

The Hindu world

There are about 700 million Hindus worldwide. Most live in India and its nearby countries. Traders spread Hinduism to parts of South-east Asia 1,000 years ago. Indians who went to Africa and the Caribbean in the nineteenth century took their religion with them. In the twentieth century many Hindus settled in Britain, Canada and the USA.

▲ Hindu worshippers

These worshippers are in a temple in Britain. Hindus came to Britain in the 1950s from countries such as India and Sri Lanka. Many more came from East Africa in the late 1960s and early 1970s. Today many young Hindus in Britain are British-born.

AN ANCIENT NAME

The word 'Hindu' was used by the ancient Persians (who lived in the area of modern-day Iran) over 2,000 years ago. They used the name to describe the people who lived east of the River Indus, in what is now Pakistan.

TIMELINE

The development of Hinduism

CE = Common Era (this refers to the same time period as AD (Anno Domini, 'in the year of our Lord') which is traditionally used in the Christian world)

BCE = Before the Common Era

C. 3000 BCE	C. 2500 BCE	C. 1500 BCE	C 1500–1000 BCE	C. 800 BCE	C. 500 BCE
Krishna appeared and spoke to Bhagavad Gita, according to Hindu texts.	The great cities of the Indus valley are at the height of their power.	The Aryan people begin to invade India, according to scholars. Hinduism begins to develop.	The *Vedas* are used by priests. The system of 4 *varnas* and 4 *ashrams* develops.	The *Upanishads* are composed.	The Buddha spreads his teaching and lays the foundations for Buddhism.

◀ Seal used by Indus valley peoples

Buddha ▶

CE1828	CE1757	CE 1600s–1700s	CE1632	CE1570s	CE1556–1605
The Brahmo Samaj (Society of God) is founded, seeking to reform Hinduism.	India starts to come under British power and becomes part of the British Empire in 1858.	Many Europeans arrive in India, mainly to trade.	Shah Jehan builds the Taj Mahal in Agra as a memorial to his wife.	The saint Tulsi Das writes the *Ram Charit Manas*, a poem based on the *Ramayana*.	The Mogul emperor Akbar the Great is emperor of India.

CE1857
First Indian war of independence against the British.

Taj Mahal

The flag of India ▶

CE1869	CE1875	CE1876	CE1897	CE1910	CE1947
Birth of Mahatma Gandhi, a great leader in India's struggle for independence.	The Arya Samaj, another Hindu reform movement, is formed.	Queen Victoria takes the title Empress of India.	The Ramakrishna Mission is established in Calcutta.	Sri Aurobindo starts a religious centre in Pondicherry, India.	India gains independence but is split into Hindu India and Muslim Pakistan.

New countries

Britain ruled India from the late eighteenth century until 1947. Most Indians were Hindus but there were also a large number of Muslims. When India gained independence, the country's Muslims called for a separate nation to be set up where they would be free to rule themselves. Their demand was granted. The western state of Punjab and the eastern state of Bengal became West and East Pakistan. East Pakistan became Bangladesh in 1971. The partition of India led to terrible violence between Hindus and Muslims and many people were forced to leave their homes.

400BCE – CE 400 Large parts of the *Ramayana* and *Mahabharata* are composed.	CE320–550 The Gupta kings rule India – a 'golden age' for Hinduism.	C. CE700–800 The Hindu Mataram kingdom is established in Java, Indonesia.	C. CE800 The great philosopher Shankara teaches about the *Upanishads*.
			C. CE900 The Chola kings rule south India. Many beautiful temples are built.
CE1526 The Muslim Mogul Empire is founded in India.	CE1469 The birth of Guru Nanak, founder of the Sikh religion. Bhakti saints popular at this time.	CE1206–1555 Muslims are powerful in the north, but a Hindu kingdom thrives in south India.	C. CE1050 Ramanuja, a Hindu philosopher, teaches devotion to a personal God, in south India.
CE1948 Mahatma Gandhi is assassinated.	CE 1950s–1960s Many Hindus leave India to live in Britain, Canada and the USA.	CE1960s / 1970s Many Hindus arrive in the UK, especially from East Africa, and establish the first temples.	

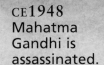

▲ Coin of the Gupta kings

◀ Mahatma Gandhi

Swastika ▶

Sign of luck ▲

In the twentieth century a version of the swastika became the symbol of the German Nazi Party. It became associated with evil. For Hindus, however, it is an ancient symbol of luck and good fortune.

HOW DID HINDUISM BEGIN?

Many Hindus believe that religion is forever and that their own tradition goes back thousands, even millions of years. Scholars say that Hinduism began over 4,000 years ago. Clay figures found in the ruins of Indus valley cities look similar to the deities (representations of God) worshipped by Hindus today.

The religion of the Indus valley people combined with the beliefs of people called the Aryans. The Aryans arrived in India from the north-west in around 1500 BCE. They worshipped many deities, mostly linked to the natural world.

Two great cities ▼

Archaeologists began excavating the Indus valley cities of Harappa and Mohenjo Daro in the 1920s. Each had a hilltop fort (see below), used as a temple and government building.

Hundreds of stone seals have been found among the ruins. Many show sacred animals such as bulls or elephants and merchants used them to mark their goods.

Seal showing a bull

▲ King or priest?

This carved stone head was found at Mohenjo Daro. It could be the head of a king, or a priest with his eyes closed in meditation.

RITUALS AND SACRIFICES

The Aryans believed that health and good harvests were dependent on the good will of God and the various deities. Their priests would throw offerings of grains, spices, butter and milk into the sacred fire. Goats and horses were sometimes sacrificed, too. As the priests performed the sacrifices, they sang hymns and chanted mantras (sacred spells). The Aryans believed that the deities could accept offerings through the flames of a fire.

Agni ▲
The carving above shows Agni, the god of fire and sacrifice. He was one of the most important Aryan deities.

◄ Indra
Indra was the most popular Aryan god, famous for his bravery and strength. He was the god of war and also of storms and thunder. His weapon was the thunderbolt. In this picture he is riding his white battle elephant.

WHAT DO HINDUS BELIEVE?

Most Hindus share the same basic beliefs, even though they do not all worship in the same way. One important teaching is reincarnation. This

means that when you die your soul is reborn in the body of another human or animal. You can be reborn many times. Hindus hope that by leading a good life they will break free of the cycle of death and rebirth and achieve salvation, or *moksha*.

◄ **Sacred river**
These Hindus are bathing in the River Ganges in India. They believe that the water of the Ganges is holy. By bathing in it they wash away their sins and come closer to achieving *moksha*.

▲ **Sacred sound**
This symbol is the sound 'Om'. Hindus recite this sound during meditation and at the beginning of prayers and mantras.

◄ Monastery schools

These boys are being educated at an *ashram*. An *ashram* is a place or community for spiritual development. The boys are taught by priests and religious teachers called *gurus*. The pupils treat their *gurus* with great respect. Adult Hindus sometimes spend time at an *ashram* to seek spiritual guidance.

A way of life ►

Hindus try to follow a sacred code of behaviour called *dharma*. This means serving God and doing their duty to family, friends and society. Religion affects everything in their daily life from working honestly to the food they eat, which is often vegetarian.

PATHS TO FOLLOW

There are four paths Hindus can follow to reach *moksha*.

- The Path of Devotion – prayer, worship and devotion to God.
- The Path of Knowledge – study and learning, with a guru's guidance.
- The Path of Right Action – acting without any thought of reward for yourself.
- The Path of Yoga – yoga and meditation.

WHICH ARE THE MAIN HINDU DEITIES?

The deities of Hinduism represent different characteristics of Brahman, the supreme soul or spirit. Brahman is all around, in everything, all the time. The three main deities are Brahma the creator, Vishnu the protector, and Shiva the destroyer.

A Hindu may worship more than one deity, though they often have a favourite or one they consider to be the supreme deity (God). Often, a family has worshipped certain deities for several generations.

◀ **Brahma**

This is a statue of Brahma, the creator of the universe and the god of wisdom. The sacred statue has four faces (although only three can be seen in this photograph). This shows that Brahma looks over the whole world – north, south, east and west. He has four arms too, in which he holds the sacred books, the prayer beads and the water pot of a holy man. Brahma, although important as the creator, is only worshipped in one place in India.

Shiva ▼

Shiva, the destroyer of the world, is often shown dancing. The dance represents the energy flowing through the world, which causes day and night, the changing seasons, death and rebirth.

Dancing Shiva

Vishnu ▲

The painting above shows Vishnu, the protector of the universe, with his wife, Lakshmi. She is the goddess of wealth and good fortune. Vishnu has come to earth nine times, in nine different forms, or *avatars*, to save the world. These include Lord Rama, Lord Krishna and Buddha. The tenth *avatar* of Vishnu is Kalki, the rider on the white horse, who is yet to come.

RIDING ANIMALS

The various deities ride on different animals. For example, Brahma rides on a swan, Vishnu rides on a giant eagle (above) and Shiva rides on a white bull called Nandi (right).

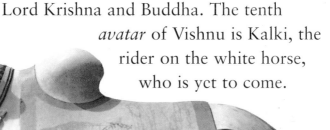

DO HINDUS WORSHIP OTHER DEITIES?

There are thousands of Hindu deities. Some are worshipped all over India, others are honoured in just one or two villages. The most worshipped are Vishnu, Shiva and the goddess Parvati.

Rama and Krishna are two of the *avatars* (forms) of Vishnu. Parvati is the wife of Shiva. Like many Hindu deities, she has other names, representing her different aspects. When she is worshipped as Kali or Durga, she is awesome and terrifying. She represents the destruction of evil and the protection of good.

◀ Rama and Sita

The picture on the left shows Rama, his wife Sita and his faithful friend, Hanuman, the monkey god. The story of Rama and Sita is told in the great poem the *Ramayana* (see pages 42-43). Rama is worshipped as an ideal human being – a great hero, a devoted husband and a just king.

SUN AND MOON

Surya, the sun god, rides across the sky each morning in his golden chariot. His wife, Ushas, is goddess of the dawn.

Surya

The silver chariot of Chandra, the moon god, crosses the sky as darkness falls.

Chandra

◀ Krishna

Krishna is usually shown with dark blue or black skin and carrying or playing a flute. He is often surrounded by cows and milkmaids, too. Krishna is famous for playing tricks on his friends and is the hero of many adventures.

Durga ▶

Durga is the warlike form of the goddess Parvati. In this picture she is riding on a fierce tiger and holding a different weapon in each of her ten hands.

Ganesha ▲

Ganesha is the son of Shiva and Parvati. Hindus pray to him before they begin anything new because he is the god who removes obstacles.

HOW DO HINDU FAMILIES LIVE?

It is traditional for Hindus to share their home with their parents, grandparents, uncles, aunts and cousins. Large family groups like this are known as joint or extended families. Children learn about their religion from their parents and grandparents. They are taught to respect the older members of their family.

◄ Family names

Hindus rarely call one another by their first names. They use special titles that describe how they are related. For example, you would call your father's younger brother *chachaji* and his wife *chachiji*. The man in the centre of the photograph on the left has just married the girl in the red sari. She will soon be getting to know his relatives because she will live in their family home.

Caste system ►

Hindus divided society into four groups called *varnas*. Traditionally, this was based on the jobs people did. The highest *varna* is the priests. Next come the warriors and nobles, and after them the merchants. Below them are the labourers, like the potters in this photograph. The present system, based on the community you are born in, is called the caste system.

Sweets

Vegetarian food ▲

Many Hindus are vegetarians because they think it is wrong to kill animals to eat. A typical meal might include a spicy vegetable dish, rice, dahl and flat bread. With their meal people drink water, sweet tea or a yoghurt drink called *lassi*.

◄ Indian sweets ▲

Many Hindus love sweets and they are often given as gifts at weddings and festivals. Milk, cheese, nuts, coconut and sugar are popular ingredients.

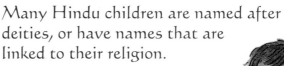

Sacred cows ▲

Hindus believe that the cow is very special because she is a mother that produces milk, a precious source of food. Wherever you go in India you will see cows wandering freely, even in the towns.

NAMES

Many Hindu children are named after deities, or have names that are linked to their religion.

Boys
Rajendra – Lord Indra
Mahesh – a name of Shiva

Girls
Devi – goddess
Vandana – worshipper

WHERE DO HINDUS WORSHIP?

For many Hindus there are no set rules about where they should worship, or when. Some Hindus set up a shrine in a room at home and worship there. They also worship in buildings called temples, or *mandirs*. Some people visit the temple every day. Others only go there at special times, such as festivals. Hindu temples are often noisy, lively places, filled with the sound of praying, chanting and singing.

◄ **Temples**
This is the entrance gateway of a temple in southern India. It is decorated with carvings of the deity. People think of the temple as the earthly home of God. This temple is dedicated to Shiva.

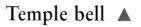

Temple bell ▲
As worshippers enter the temple, they ring the bell to announce their arrival.

Street shrines ▶

On many street corners there are small shrines like this one, where Hindus can stop to worship on their way to work or school. They might leave an offering of flowers or sweets for the deity. This shrine is dedicated to Shiva. You can see the white bull Nandi in the bottom left corner.

MORE TEMPLES

The only temple in India dedicated to Brahma is in Pushkar, in western India. In southern India, at Mahabalipuram, there is a group of very beautiful stone temples. They are 1,400 years old.
The town is still famous for the skill of its sculptors.

Temples at Mahabalipuram

◀ Worship at home

The photograph on the left shows a shrine in a Hindu home. It is dedicated to Saraswati, the goddess of art and music and the wife of Brahma. The brass pots on the floor contain leaves, flowers and sweets, which the family will offer to the goddess for her blessing.

HOW DO HINDUS WORSHIP?

There is no set time when Hindus should visit the temple – but mornings and evenings are most important. Before they enter the building, they take off their shoes. Women often cover their heads, to show respect. Hindus go to the temple to take *darshan* of the deity as well as for group worship. *Darshan* means a 'seeing' of the image or statue in the inner sanctum that shows the presence of the deity.

▲ **The inner sanctum**
A priest sits near the image of the deity in the inner sanctum, the holiest part of the temple. Only the priest is allowed to get so close to the sacred image.

◀ **Temple offerings**

Outside the temple, worshippers can buy offerings of flowers, fruit, incense and coloured powder at stalls like this one. They give their offerings to the priest and he presents them to the temple deity to be blessed. Then he hands them back to the worshipper, to carry the deity's blessing back to them. This ceremony is part of *puja*.

In the temple ▶

These worshippers are waiting for a *darshana* (sight) of the god Hanuman. They are holding offerings of flower garlands and small lamps. As part of their worship they circle the shrine. They always walk in a clockwise direction to keep their right sides facing towards the god and the inner sanctum.

Water pot

Garland

MANTRA

This short prayer is called the Gayatri Mantra. It is chanted three times a day:

'We meditate upon the brilliance and glory of the god of the sun, who lights up the heavens and the earth. May he inspire us and bless us.'

WHO ARE HINDU HOLY MEN?

Hindu holy men include priests, *gurus* and *sannyasins*. A *sannyasin* is a person who has given up his home, family and posessions to lead a life of prayer and meditation. Some holy men wander from place to place and rely on local people to give them food and shelter. Others live on an *ashram* and learn from a *guru,* or teacher.

Holy man ▶

This holy man, or *sadhu*, is a follower of Shiva. The cloth he is wearing around his waist is of a colour called saffron, which is a holy colour. He is meditating on the banks of the River Ganges. Many Hindus worship not only God but also holy men, especially *gurus*, and dedicate shrines to them.

HOLY WORDS

These are some words spoken by famous Hindu holy men:

'I have nothing new to teach the world. Truth and non-violence are as old as the hills.'
Mahatma Gandhi

'A person who accepts a gift from the gods and does not repay it is a thief.'
Sri Aurobindo

Ramakrishna ▼

A holy man called Ramakrishna taught that all religions were equal. He believed in Jesus Christ and in Muhammad, the founder of Islam, as well as in the Hindu gods. This temple belongs to the Ramakrishna Mission, which spread Ramakrishna's message.

Yoga and meditation ▼

Many Hindus use yoga exercises and meditation. They train their bodies and minds to achieve *moksha*. Some people concentrate hard on a pattern to help them focus their minds. These patterns are called *yantras*.

Priests ▲

Every temple has its own priest *(pujari)*, who looks after the image of the temple deity and performs the *puja* (ritual worship). Most Hindus have their own family priest, who comes to their home to carry out important ceremonies.

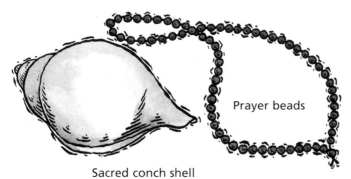

Prayer beads

Sacred conch shell

Yantra

WHICH ARE THE HINDUS' SACRED BOOKS?

The *Vedas* are the oldest of the Hindus' sacred books. They date from the time of the Aryans and are over 3,000 years old. Another important collection of teachings is the *Upanishads*. Hindus believe that a group of wise men heard the words of the *Upanishads* and the *Vedas* directly from God.

The *Mahabharata* and the *Ramayana* are two long poems. These were also made up long ago and people learned them by heart. The words were passed down from one generation to another.

The *Upanishads* ▶

The photograph on the right shows words from the *Upanishads* carved on the wall of a temple in Varanasi, India. The *Upanishads* focus on the relationship between the *atman* (soul) and Brahman (the Supreme). These sacred teachings date from around 800 BCE.

श्रीलक्ष्मीनारायण

एकही ईश्वर के अनेक नाम
स ब्रह्मा स शिवः सेन्द्रः सोऽक्षरः परमः स्वराट् ।
स एव विष्णुः स प्राणः स कालोऽग्निः स चन्द्रमाः ॥ (केवल्य उप. १/८)
सर्वशक्तिमान् और समस्त जगत् का प्रकाशकयह परमात्मा ही ब्रह्मा (सृष्टि-कर्ता) है वही शिव रुद्र
(विनाशक शक्ति) है, वही विष्णु (पालन करने वाली शक्ति) है वही इन्द्र है, अविनाशी है वही सर्वव्यापक
है, वही जगत् का जीवनाधार है वही काल है, अग्नि है, और चन्द्रमा है ।
He is one and only one God
THAT ALMIGHTY, ALLPERVADING GOD IS BRAHMA, THE CREATIVE FORM,
VISHNU THE PROTECTIVE FORM AND SHIVA, THE DESTRUCTIVE FORM. HE IS
INDRA; HE IS IMMORTAL; HE IS SELF-EXISTENT AND SELF-EFFULGENT.
HE IS LIFE-FORM, HE IS TIME, HE IS FIRE AND HE IS MOON. (K. UPANISHAD 1/8)

Bhagavad Gita

The *Bhagavad Gita* is the most important and popular part of the *Mahabharata*. The *Mahabharata* tells the story of a war between two royal families, the Kauravas and the Pandavas, who are cousins. They both want to control the kingdom of Hastinapura, but the Pandavas are its rightful rulers.

The *Bhagavad Gita*, the 'Song of the Lord', is set on the battlefield. The painting shows Arjuna, one of the Pandavas, in his chariot. Lord Krishna is his charioteer. Arjuna tells Krishna how sad he feels because he is about to fight his cousins. Krishna tells him to control his emotions and do his duty as a warrior. Acting selflessly is the way to achieve *moksha*. Arjuna follows Krishna's advice and eventually the Kaurava army is destroyed.

SANSKRIT

Sanskrit is the ancient language of the Aryans. It is the language that was used when the *Vedas* and the *Upanishads* were written down. Sanskrit is not much spoken now although it is still studied by priests. Hindi, the modern language of India, developed from it.

The *Ramayana*

The *Ramayana* tells the story of Rama and Sita (you can read the story on pages 42–43). The poem was made up over 2,000 years ago but the most famous version was written in the 1570s by Tulsi Das, who is shown in the picture on the left. It has also been made into a television series.

WHICH ARE THE HINDUS' SACRED PLACES?

Many sacred places are connected to events in the lives of various deities and the many Hindu saints. Some are famous for their beauty or because people have been miraculously healed there. Every year millions of Hindus set off on journeys to visit sacred places. These journeys are called pilgrimages. People might go on a pilgrimage to ask God or specific deities to grant them a special request, or to give thanks to them. Sometimes people walk for many days to reach a place of pilgrimage.

◀ Holy places

This map shows some of the holiest places in India. Hindus believe they can pass beyond this world to obtain *moksha* at some of these sites.

Varanasi ▶

The city of Varanasi is the holiest place of pilgrimage. Hindu legends say that Shiva chose Varanasi as his home on earth. Most Hindus believe Varanasi is the best place to die and many go there to scatter the ashes of their dead relatives in the River Ganges. Pilgrims wash away their sins in its holy waters.

◄ Bathing fairs

Every twelve years, a great fair is held at Allahabad. Over two million pilgrims come to bathe at the point where the River Ganges, the River Yamuna and the mythical River Saraswati flow together. This type of fair is called a *kumbha mela*.

LEGEND OF THE GANGES

There was once a king who begged Shiva to let the magical River Ganges fall to earth. Shiva agreed to his request, but to make sure the earth would not shatter under the weight of the water, he caught the river in his hair. Then he let it flow down gently from the Himalayas.

Rameshwaram ▲

This is the Ramanathaswamy temple on the island of Rameshwaram in south India. Rama is said to have worshipped here after his battle with Ravana (see pages 42–43). It is an important place of pilgrimage.

Sacred mountains ►

The Himalayan mountains that stretch across northern India are the highest mountains in the world. Many of them are holy places. These pilgrims are making the difficult journey to Gangotri, the source of the River Ganges.

WHAT ARE THE MAIN HINDU FESTIVALS?

Hindus hold festivals to celebrate important events in the lives of their deities and saints. Festivals are also linked to the changing seasons and to harvest time. There are far too many festivals for everyone to celebrate all of them but most Hindus celebrate Diwali, Holi and Dussehra. For Hindus living outside India, festivals are an important way for children to learn about their religion and a time for families and friends to get together.

◄ Local festivals

These women are preparing offerings. Local festivals celebrate the harvest or honour the village deities. Some festivals, such as the kite-flying festival in western India, are not religious – they are just good fun.

Kite

Diwali ►

Diwali is the Hindu festival of lights and it is celebrated in late October or early November. People light small oil lamps and place them by their doors and windows to guide Rama back home (see the story on pages 42–43). They enjoy firework displays and delicious food. They also give each other cards and presents.

Dussehra ▶

The Dussehra festival is held in October. For most Hindus it is a celebration of Rama's victory over the demon king, Ravana. Giant models of Ravana are used in a performance of the story.

Holi ▲

Holi is the liveliest and messiest festival of the year. It is held in March to celebrate the coming of spring. People put on old clothes and pelt each other with coloured water and powder. After a bath and change of clothes they visit their relatives to wish them happy Holi.

Raksha Bandhan ▶

At Raksha Bandhan brothers and sisters show their affection for each other. Girls tie bracelets called *rakhis* around their brothers' wrists. Boys give their sisters a gift.

Rakhi bracelets

HINDU CALENDAR

HINDU MONTH	
Chaitra	March–April
Vaisakha	April–May
Jyaishtha	May–June
Ashadha	June–July
Shravana	July–August
Bhadra	August–September
Ashvina	September–October
Karttika	October–November
Margashirsha	November–December
Pausha	December–January
Magha	January–February
Phalguna	February–March

WHAT ARE THE MOST IMPORTANT TIMES IN A HINDU'S LIFE?

Hindus mark important times in their lives with ceremonies called *samskaras*. These begin even before a baby is born, with prayers for it to be healthy and happy. Once the baby arrives there are ceremonies to mark its birth, the first time it sees the sun and its first haircut.

Getting married is another important occasion marked with a *samskara*. The final ceremonies take place when a person dies and is cremated.

Horoscope ▶

The picture on the right is a horoscope for a baby boy. It shows the position of the stars and planets at the exact moment of the baby's birth. A priest draws up the horoscope and uses it to work out what may happen to the baby in the future. This is done at the baby's naming ceremony, which usually takes place ten days after its birth.

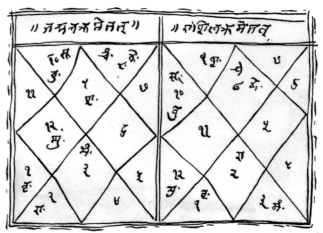

Baby boy's horoscope

▼ Sacred thread

Boys from the top three *varnas* – Brahmins, Kshatriyas and Vaishyas – go through the sacred thread ceremony when they are about nine or ten years old. A priest loops a cotton thread over the boy's left shoulder and under his right arm. This marks the start of his adult life. He can now begin to study the holy books and take more responsibility within the family.

◀ A Hindu wedding ▼

A Hindu wedding lasts for several days and often 15 rituals are performed. In the photograph on the left the bride and groom are exchanging flower garlands. The bride below is wearing beautiful jewellery. The groom will give her a special necklace.

STAGES OF LIFE

A Hindu man's life is traditionally divided into four stages (ashrams):
Brahmachari – Life as a student
Grihastha – Married life
Vanaprastha – Retirement
Sannyas – Life as a wandering holy man

Death and cremation ▶

Hindus are almost always cremated. The person's eldest son or male relation lights the fire while a priest chants from the holy books. Burning the body helps the soul give up attachment to the body and move onto the next life. If possible, people scatter the ashes of their dead relative in the River Ganges.

WHAT IS TRADITIONAL HINDU MEDICINE?

Traditional Hindu medicine is called Ayurveda, which means the 'science of long life'. Ayurvedic medicine has changed very little in thousands of years.

Ayurvedic doctors are called *vaidyas*. They believe that the body contains three 'humours' – bile, wind and mucus. When people become ill, it is because they have too much or too little of one of these humours. The *vaidya's* treatment brings the humours back into balance again. Eating healthy foods, taking exercise and doing yoga are also important ways of keeping the body's humours balanced.

Sacred herb ▼

The girl below is looking after a tulsi bush. Tulsi is a herb and it is believed to be very good for healing. People think of it as a sacred plant, linked to Vishnu. They often plant tulsi bushes to bring them good luck.

▲ Ayurvedic chemist's shop

This chemist's shop in western India is run by the government. It sells Ayurvedic medicines. Many people prefer Ayurvedic medicines to modern drugs, although some use a mixture of the two. There are hundreds of different ingredients in Ayurvedic medicines, including plants, herbs, spices and oils.

Coriander

Cardamom

NATURAL MEDICINES

The herbs and spices shown on this page are all used to treat different health problems.

Coriander – good for the digestion and skin problems
Cardamom – good for the heart and lungs
Black pepper – good for treating loss of appetite and to reduce swelling
Ginger – good for headaches, sore throats and colds

Pepper

Ginger

Healthy living

Here is a suggested Ayurvedic routine for a healthy life.

- Wake up early, before sunrise.

- Go to the toilet regularly.

- Have a bath every morning.

- Eat breakfast before 8 a.m.

- Wash your hands before and after eating.

- Eat slowly and in silence.

- Take a short walk 15 minutes after a meal.

- Go to sleep before 10 p.m.

Street seller ▶

This street seller has spread out dried plants, roots and herbs on the pavement. The metal bar in front of him is his weighing scale.

WHAT IS HINDU ART LIKE?

A lot of Hindu art is linked to religion. There are many sacred statues of the deities. Often these are made for the inner sanctum of the temple or a family shrine. They are a symbol of God's presence on earth. Hindu artists also produce beautiful paintings and carvings that show scenes and stories from the sacred books. Many of the tools used by artists and sculptors have not changed in hundreds of years.

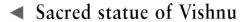

◀ Sacred statue of Vishnu

This statue of Vishnu is carved from ivory. It shows him sitting on the coils of a serpent while he waits for Brahma to create the world. In his four arms he holds the signs of his divinity and power: a conch shell, a lotus flower, a club and a discus (spinning disc used as a weapon).

Symbol of Shiva ▼

The picture below shows a *lingam*, carved in stone or marble. It is a symbol of Shiva's presence and power. In temples dedicated to Shiva there is often a *lingam* in the inner sanctum instead of a sacred statue of the god.

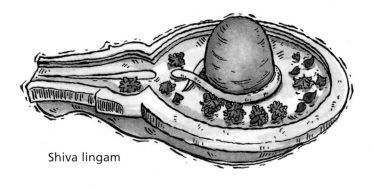

Shiva lingam

Arctic Circle

N
W E
S

Montreal

New York

Washington DC

ATLANTIC OCEAN

11 THE BAHAMAS

Havana
12 CUBA
14 HAITI
15 DOMINICAN REPUBLIC
13 JAMAICA

16 PUERTO RICO

17 LEEWARD ISLANDS

CARIBBEAN SEA

18 WINDWARD ISLANDS

19 TRINIDAD AND TOBAGO

HONDURAS

8 NICARAGUA

9 COSTA RICA
10 PANAMA

Can you find these pictures on the map?

fruit

bear

cactus

computers

canyon

wheat

Hello, I'm from Jamaica.

I'm Canadian, from Canada.

Statue of Liberty

Can you find these countries?

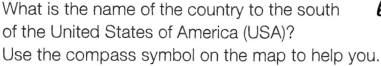

What is the name of the country to the south of the United States of America (USA)?
Use the compass symbol on the map to help you.

Animal

Bear

Bears live in forests all over the USA, from Alaska in the north-west, down through the Rocky Mountains to central Mexico. Bears are omnivores – they eat plants and meat.

Plant

Cactus

Cacti grow in dry deserts. They store milky water in their stems. Their thorny spines stop animals from getting close enough to drink this water and protect them from damage.

Industry

Computers

Most of the largest computer technology companies in the world are on the west coast of the USA, in Seattle and San Francisco. Can you find these cities on the map?

Did you know?
Canada is the second largest country in the world.
The largest is Russia (pages 18-19).

Natural Feature

Canyon

A canyon is a deep valley that has been cut through the rock by a fast flowing river. The Colorado River started making the Grand Canyon millions of years ago.

Monument

Statue of Liberty

This huge monument is in the entrance to New York harbour. The seven spikes on her crown represent the seven oceans and the seven continents of the world.

Crop

Wheat

Wheat is a very important crop. It is used to make bread, cakes and pasta. Large crops of wheat are grown in the centre of Canada and the USA.

Food

Fruit

Oranges from Florida, USA, mangoes and other tropical fruit from Guatemala and bananas from the Caribbean islands are delicious to eat and good to export.

South America

CARIBBEAN SEA

ATLANTIC OCEAN

PACIFIC OCEAN

Equator

Tropic of Capricorn

N
E
S
W

Caracas

2 VENEZUELA

Orinoco River

1 COLOMBIA

ECUADOR
13

12 PERU

Lima

Machu Picchu

Angel Falls

3 GUYANA

4 SURINAME

5 FRENCH GUIANA

Amazon River

Madeira River

Amazon Rainforest

Amazon River

11 BOLIVIA

Atacama Desert

MOUNTAINS

7 PARAGUAY

8

Tocantins River

São Francisco River

Brasília

Rio de Janeiro

Paraná River

6 BRAZIL

South America

Look at the map of South America.
Can you name two countries beginning with C?

Monument

Cathedral

The capital city of Brazil is
Brasilia. It is a modern city
with a very modern cathedral.
The pillars of the roof look as
if they are reaching up
to the sky.

Food

Beef

There are more cows than people
on the grasslands of Argentina,
Brazil and Uruguay! Along with
Paraguay, these countries export
beef all over the world.

Industry

Oil

Oil is drilled from under the ground
or under the sea. We use oil for
energy, for example to run cars
and heat houses. Oil drilling is
the main industry
of Venezuela.

Did you know?
The Atacama Desert in Chile is said to be the driest place on earth.

Natural Feature

Rainforest

The Amazon is the largest tropical rainforest in the world. The canopy is so thick that when it rains, it takes about ten minutes for the water to reach the ground.

Animal

Llama

Llamas are related to camels. They can carry goods through difficult areas like deserts and mountains. Their wool is used for clothes, rugs and ropes. Their dung is used for fires.

Did you know that coffee is a bean grown on a bush?

Crop

Coffee

The coffee bean is red when it is ripe. To make the popular drink, the bean is washed and dried and then roasted. A lot of coffee is grown in Brazil and Colombia and exported all over the world.

Plant

Orchid

Orchids like the hot, wet climate of the rainforest. They have roots that take what they need from the air rather than the soil so they can grow on trees.

Europe

1 ICELAND

ATLANTIC OCEAN

Faroe Islands (Denmark)

2 NORWAY

3 SWEDEN

4 DENMARK

BALTIC SEA

6 RUS

SCOTLAND

NORTHERN IRELAND

37 UNITED KINGDOM

WALES

ENGLAND

36 IRELAND

NORTH SEA

London
Thames River

Berlin

28 POLAND

38 NETHERLANDS

39 BELGIUM

40 LUXEMBOURG

41 GERMANY

Rhine River

29 CZECH REPUBLIC

27 SLOVAKIA

30 AUSTRIA

26 HUNGARY

Paris

35 FRANCE

BAY OF BISCAY

PYRENEES

Rhône River

42 SWITZERLAND

Mont Blanc

ALPS

25 SLOVENIA

24 CROATIA

22 BOSNIA & HERZEGOVINA

SER

21 MONTENEGRO

Po River

31 ITALY

Corsica (France)

Rome

18 ALBANIA

M

GR

Tagus River

Madrid

34 PORTUGAL

Lisbon

33 SPAIN

Balearic Islands (Spain)

Sardinia (Italy)

MEDITERRANEAN SEA

Sicily (Italy)

32 MALTA

Can you find these pictures on the map?

cheese

sheep

pine tree

cars

tomatoes

river

castle

Good morning. Where are you from?

I'm Greek. I'm from Greece.

Can you find this country?

Europe

Can you name the country to the west of Spain? Use the compass on the map to help you.

Sheep

Sheep are bred for their fleece (which is made into wool) and their meat. Female sheep are called ewes and males are called rams. A group of sheep is a flock. They eat grass and plants.

Cheese

Cheese is made from cow, goat or sheep milk. France and Italy are famous for their cheese.

Cars

Some of the most well-known cars in the world are made in Germany. Can you name one make beginning with V? Its name means 'people's car'.

Did you know?

The highest mountain in the Alps is Mont Blanc (white mountain). It is on the border of France, Italy and Switzerland.

Natural Feature

River

The Danube River flows from Germany to the Black Sea. Millions of people drink its water and it's so big that even large ships can travel down it. Can you find it on the map?

Monument

Castle

In ancient times, the kings and nobles of Europe built castles to defend their cities and countries against their enemies. Many of these castles are now ruins but are popular tourist attractions.

Tomatoes came to Europe from Peru (page 6).

Crop

Plant

Pine tree

Pine forests cover mountains and hills from Norway to Greece. Pine trees are evergreen so their needle-like leaves stay on the tree all year. Pine wood is used for building and furniture.

Tomatoes

Tomatoes are a very important crop in the south of Italy. They are grown to eat fresh or made into sauce to eat with spaghetti or pizza. Tomatoes are also tinned to keep them fresh.

Africa

N E S W

MEDITERRANEAN SEA

Tropic of Cancer

RED SEA

INDIAN OCEAN

Equator

Nile River

Niger River

Congo River

Sahara Desert

Cairo ■
EGYPT

LIBYA

NIGER

CHAD

SUDAN

SOUTH SUDAN

ERITREA

DJIBOUTI

SOMALIA

ETHIOPIA

KENYA
Mount Kenya
Nairobi ■
Mount Kilimanjaro
TANZANIA

UGANDA
Lake Victoria

RWANDA
BURUNDI

CENTRAL AFRICAN REPUBLIC

CAMEROON

EQUATORIAL GUINEA

GABON

REPUBLIC OF THE CONGO

DEMOCRATIC REPUBLIC OF THE CONGO

SAO TOME AND PRINCIPE

NIGERIA

BENIN

TOGO

GHANA

IVORY COAST

LIBERIA

BURKINA FASO

SIERRA LEONE

GUINEA

GUINEA BISSAU

GAMBIA

SENEGAL

MAURITANIA

MALI

WESTERN SAHARA

MOROCCO

ALGERIA

TUNISIA

Canary Islands (Spain)

CAPE VERDE

SEYCHELLES

1 MOROCCO
2 TUNISIA
3 ALGERIA
4 LIBYA
5 EGYPT
7 MAURITANIA
8 SENEGAL
9 GAMBIA
10 GUINEA BISSAU
11 MALI
12 GUINEA
13 BURKINA FASO
14 SIERRA LEONE
15 IVORY COAST
16 LIBERIA
17 GHANA
18 TOGO
19 BENIN
20 NIGERIA
21 NIGER
22 CHAD
23 SUDAN
24 SOUTH SUDAN
25 ERITREA
26 DJIBOUTI
27 SOMALIA
28 ETHIOPIA
29 CENTRAL AFRICAN REPUBLIC
30 CAMEROON
31 EQUATORIAL GUINEA
32 SAO TOME AND PRINCIPE
33 UGANDA
34 KENYA
35 GABON
36 REPUBLIC OF THE CONGO
37 RWANDA
38 BURUNDI
39 DEMOCRATIC REPUBLIC OF THE CONGO
40 TANZANIA
53 CAPE VERDE
55 SEYCHELLES

Africa

Can you name the country to the east of Namibia? Use the compass to help you.

Did you know chocolate is made from the cocoa bean?

Elephant

Elephants used to roam across most of Africa. Now they are threatened by poachers who kill them for their tusks. The tourist industry helps to protect the elephants.

Cocoa/Chocolate

Cocoa trees grow in west Africa, particularly in the Ivory Coast and Ghana. Large pods sprout from the tree trunk.
The large seeds inside the pod are dried and made into chocolate.

Tourist

Tourists visit Kenya to see wild animals and Egypt to see ancient ruins. They travel to Morocco to trek in the desert and lie on the beach. Can you find these countries on the map?

16

Did you know?
The Equator divides the earth into the Northern and Southern Hemispheres. Can you find it on the map?

Waterfall

Mosi-oa-Tunya is also known as the Victoria Falls. It means 'the smoke which thunders' and describes the spray and noise of the huge waterfall. It is on the Zambezi River along the border of Zimbabwe and Zambia.

Monument

Pyramids

Ancient Egyptians built the pyramids as tombs for their pharaohs. They are in the desert outside Cairo, the capital city of Egypt.

Plant

Crop

Maize

Maize or corn is a very important food crop in Africa, even though it needs good rainfall. Ripe maize cobs are ground to a flour and then made into porridge.

Date palm

Date palms are found in oases – parts of the desert where there is water. They need very hot daytime temperatures and warm nights to grow. Dates are the fruit of the palm.

Asia

ARCTIC OCEAN

N W E S

Ob' River
Yenis River

2 RUSSIA

BLACK SEA

1 TURKEY

3 GEORGIA

CASPIAN SEA

Gobi Desert

21 KAZAKHSTAN

20 UZBEKISTAN

4 ARMENIA

5 AZERBAIJAN

22 KYRGYZSTAN

MEDITERRANEAN SEA

6 SYRIA

19 TURKMENISTAN

17 IRAQ

LEBANON 7

Tehran

23 TAJIKISTAN

Mount Everest

ISRAEL 8

9 JORDAN

Euphrates River
Tigris River

18 IRAN

24 AFGHANISTAN

HIMALAYAS

16 KUWAIT

25 PAKISTAN

29 NEPAL

31 BHUTAN

BAHRAIN 15

14 QATAR

RED SEA

10 SAUDI ARABIA

13 UNITED ARAB EMIRATES

New Delhi

Indus River

Ganges River

30 BANGLADESH

12 OMAN

27 INDIA

32 MYANMA (BURM

11 YEMEN

ARABIAN SEA

BAY OF BENGAL

28 SRI LANKA

26 MALDIVES

INDIAN OCEAN

Can you find these pictures on the map?

rice

bamboo

tiger

Great Wall

mountain

tea

space exploration

Can you find these countries and their capital cities?

Asia

An ocean is a large sea. Can you name the two oceans on the map?

Animal

Tiger

Tigers are very large, very heavy, very loud and very fast! They live in hot countries like India but also very cold areas like northern China.

Food

Rice

Rice is the seed of a grass. The seedlings are planted in flooded fields. It is the main food for people in south Asia and China.

Industry

Space exploration

Because very few people live on the steppe of Kazakhstan, rockets, satellites and space stations from many countries in the world are launched into space from here.

Natural Feature

Mountain

The highest mountain in the world is in the Himalayas. This is the mountain range in the centre of Asia. Do you know its name?

Monument

Great Wall

The ancient Chinese built a wall to keep out their enemies to the north. It was built of stone, wood and mud. Tourists now enjoy visiting this great monument.

Plant

Tea

The tea bush grows high in the hills of India and China. It needs a lot of rain. The leaves are picked and then dried to make the tea we drink.

Crop

Bamboo

Bamboo is a very large grass, more like a tree. It grows very fast and can grow the height of a child over a day and a night! It is used to make buildings, paper, food and even bicycles.

N
W · E
S

Mariana
Islands
(USA)

11
MARSHALL
ISLANDS

9
FEDERATED STATES OF
MICRONESIA

8
PALAU

10
NAURU

7
PAPUA NEW
GUINEA

■ Port Moresby

6
SOLOMON
ISLANDS

1
AUSTRALIA

GREAT BARRIER REEF

GREAT DIVIDING RANGE

New
Caledonia
(France)

5
VANUATU

Tropic of Capricorn

■ Perth

Uluru

Darling River

Murray River

■ Sydney

■ Canberra

■ Melbourne

TASMAN
SEA

2
NEW
ZEALAND

■ Welling

Tasmania
(Australia)

SOUTHERN ALPS

SOUTHERN OCEAN

22

Can you find these pictures on the map?

butter

kangaroo

coconut palm

sugar cane

gold mining

desert

Sydney Harbour Bridge

Hello, I'm Australian.

I'm from the Solomon Islands.

Can you find these countries?

Tropic of Cancer

Hawaii (USA)

PACIFIC OCEAN

Equator

12 KIRIBATI

14 TUVALU

Tokelau (NZ)

Wallis and Futuna Islands (France)

13 SAMOA

American Samoa (USA)

Cook Islands (NZ)

Tahiti (France)

FIJI

3 TONGA

Niue (NZ)

French Polynesia (France)

Pitcairn Islands (UK)

Kermadec Islands (NZ)

23

Australia, New Zealand

There are around 1,000 islands in the Pacific Ocean. Can you find four groups of islands beginning with T?

Animal

Kangaroo

Kangaroos live in Australia and the island of Papua New Guinea. They can jump very high on their strong back legs. They carry their young in a pouch.

Food

Butter

Butter is made from creamy cow's milk. New Zealand has good grass and weather for cows, not too hot or cold, not too wet or dry. Most New Zealand butter is exported to other countries.

Industry

Gold mining

Gold is a metal found in rocks. In Western Australia the rock is mined using very large diggers. Gold is used as money, to make jewellery and even on space craft.

and the Pacific Islands

Desert

The centre of Australia is mostly arid land and desert as it gets very little rain. Few people live in the desert. It is very hot during the day but can get quite cold at night.

Monument

Sydney Harbour Bridge

Sydney is one of the largest cities in Australia, but it is not the capital. The city is built around a big bay of water. The Sydney Harbour Bridge crosses the bay, linking one part of the city to another.

Crop

Sugar cane

Sugar cane is a large grass. It grows in Australia and the Pacific Islands. Sugar is the juice in the stalk. The stalks are crushed and heated in a sugar mill or factory to extract the sugar.

Plant

Coconut palm

Coconut palms grow best just north and south of the Equator, particularly in the Pacific islands. The coconuts, the fruit, are used for food, the leaves for roofs and the trunks for building houses.

Antarctica

SOUTHERN OCEAN

N
W   E
S

towards Africa

Antarctic Circle

SCOTIA SEA

towards
South
America

WEDDELL
SEA

ANTARCTICA

● South Pole

TRANSANTARCTIC MOUNTAINS

AMUNDSEN
SEA

Can you see
the South
Pole?

ROSS
SEA

SOUTHERN OCEAN

towards
Australia

Can you find these pictures on the map?

ice

penguin

research laboratory

scientists

Antarctica

Did you know?
Antarctica is the coldest continent on earth. It's also the driest and windiest. Brrrr!

Antarctica is bigger than Europe and almost twice the size of Australia.

Natural Feature

Ice

Most of Antarctica is covered with very thick ice. It has the largest amount of ice on earth and this is increasing. Certain animals and plants have learned to live on the ice.

Animal

Penguin

Penguins have more feathers than other birds to keep them warm. Male emperor penguins hold their partner's eggs on their feet away from the cold ice. They can't fly but they use their flippers to swim under the ice to hunt for fish.

Industry

Research

The only humans living in Antartica are scientists. They come from lots of different countries in the world to study the ice and the climate. They have special buildings where they live and work.

The Arctic Ocean

N W E S

PACIFIC OCEAN

GULF OF ALASKA

BERING SEA

SEA OF OKHOTSK

Arctic Circle

2 USA

THE ARCTIC OCEAN

● North Pole

3 RUSSIA

Yenisi River

1 CANADA

Baffin Island (Canada)

8 GREENLAND

Svalbard (Norway)

GREENLAND SEA

Ob River

■ Nuuk

7 ICELAND

NORWEGIAN SEA

6 NORWAY

5 SWEDEN

4 FINLAND

ATLANTIC OCEAN

Can you see the North Pole?

Can you find these pictures on the map?

seaweed

polar bear

goose

fish

The Arctic Ocean

Can you find Russia, Greenland and Canada on the map?

Did you know?
The Arctic is an ocean within the Arctic Circle. It is surrounded by Russia, Greenland, the USA and Canada.

Goose

In the summer geese live in the Arctic. In the winter, when they migrate south to warmer areas, they fly in V-shaped flocks. Have you seen geese flying like this?

Plant

Seaweed

For most of the winter the Arctic is dark, even in the daytime. Although plants need light to grow, Arctic seaweed grows well in cold water with very little sunlight.

Food

Fish

The Arctic Ocean is full of fish – large fish like whales and smaller fish like cod. These fish provide food for seals and polar bears. Much of the fish we eat comes from the Arctic.

Animal

Polar bear

Polar bears are the largest and longest bears on earth. They swim well and they stand on large pieces of floating ice while they hunt for seals to eat.

Answers

p.4   What is the name of the country to the south of the United States of America (USA)? **Mexico**

p.8   Can you name two countries beginning with C? **Colombia and Chile.**

p.12   Can you name the country to the west of Spain? **Portugal**

       Can you name one make of car beginning with V? Its name means 'people's car'. **Volkswagen**

p.16   Can you name the country to the east of Namibia? **Botswana**

p.20   Can you name the two oceans on the map? **Indian Ocean and Pacific Ocean.**

p.21   The highest mountain in the world is in the Himalayas. Do you know its name? **Mount Everest**

p.24   Can you find four groups of islands beginning with T? **Tonga, Tuvalu, Tokelau, Tahiti**

List of countries

North and Central America p.2-3

1   Canada
2   United States of America
3   Mexico
4   Guatemala
5   Belize
6   Honduras
7   El Salvador
8   Nicaragua
9   Costa Rica
10   Panama
11   The Bahamas
12   Cuba
13   Jamaica
14   Haiti
15   Dominican Republic
16   Puerto Rico
17   Leeward Islands
18   Windward Islands
19   Trinidad and Tobago
Alaska (USA)
Hawaii (USA)

South America p.6-7

1   Colombia
2   Venezuela
3   Guyana
4   Suriname
5   French Guiana
6   Brazil
7   Paraguay
8   Uruguay
9   Argentina
10   Chile
11   Bolivia
12   Peru
13   Ecuador
Falkland Islands (UK)

Europe p.10-11

1   Iceland
2   Norway
3   Sweden
4   Denmark
5   Finland
6   Russia
7   Estonia
8   Latvia
9   Lithuania
10   Belarus
11   Ukraine
12   Moldova
13   Romania
14   Bulgaria
15   Turkey
16   Cyprus
17   Greece
18   Albania
19   Macedonia
20   Kosovo
21   Montenegro
22   Bosnia & Herzegovina
23   Serbia
24   Croatia
25   Slovenia
26   Hungary
27   Slovakia
28   Poland
29   Czech Republic
30   Austria
31   Italy
32   Malta
33   Spain
34   Portugal
35   France
36   Ireland
37   United Kingdom
38   Netherlands
39   Belgium
40   Luxembourg
41   Germany
42   Switzerland
Balearic Islands (Spain)
Corsica (France)
Sardinia (Italy)
Sicily (Italy)
Crete (Greece)
Faroe Islands (Denmark)

Africa p.14-15

1   Morocco
2   Tunisia
3   Algeria
4   Libya
5   Egypt
6   Western Sahara
7   Mauritania
8   Senegal
9   Gambia
10   Guinea Bissau

31

Glossary

Arid - dry land or climate. An area with little rainfall where it is too dry for plants to grow.

Bay - part of the coastline where the land curves in to surround an area of water.

Canopy - the tops of trees in a forest. The branches and leaves are so close together that they form a sort of cover.

Canyon - a deep gorge or valley in the earth, with cliffs either side, carved out by a river.

Capital city - the most important city in the country. It is usually where the government is based and from where the country is run.

Climate - the general weather conditions in a particular place.

Continent - a big mass of land and surrounding islands. There are seven continents in the world.

Crop - plants grown for food, usually in large quantities.

Equator - an imaginary line around the middle of the world. It is an equal distance between the North Pole and South Pole and separates the Northern Hemisphere from the Southern Hemisphere.

Exportation - sending items to another country to be sold there.

Hemisphere - half of a sphere. The top and bottom halves of the globe.

Industry - a way of making money, often involving factories or machinery. A business.

Landmark - a feature in the landscape that can usually be seen from a distance.

Latitude - a set distance north or south of the equator. The tropics of Cancer and Capricorn and the Arctic and Antarctic Circles are latitude lines.

Migration - the movement of animals or people from one place to another. Migration of animals is usually linked to the seasons.

Mining - removing material from the ground for use in industry.

Monument - a large construction that is important or interesting.

Mountain range - a chain of mountains.

Natural feature - a part of the landscape not made by humans.

Oasis - area in the desert where there is water. Plants are able to grow here.

Omnivore - an animal or human that eats meat and plants.

Pharaoh - an Egyptian ruler.

Poacher - someone who illegally hunts animals.

Seedling - a young plant grown from a seed.

Steppe - a large area of grassland.

Tourist attraction - a place lots of people choose to visit, often on holiday.